Schizophrenia

It'll Follow You
Wherever You Go

I have changed the names of
real life characters in this book.

ISBN978108210670

Acknowledgments

Many thanks to everyone who has
helped and seen me through my journey of
paranoid schizophrenia. To all the services
that have been there for me, Clubhouse,
Mountcroft Resource Centre, Lancashire County
Council and Age Concern, to mention a few.

My friends and family who have all seen
and shared my journey in the same way.

To my wife for being here for me.

I dedicate this book to my brother,

Andrew Debar

Schizophrenia

It'll Follow You
Wherever You Go

Table of Contents

Chapter 1

Psychosis

"That's him," She said.

"He's on the street fighter's list because he can't stand up for himself."

I heard one girl say as I walked my dog along the promenade. Another girl was pushing a pram. Their conversation went on...

"No! I won't go out with him as well." The other girl replied.

"Oh! But he's not a bad lad really; he's SAS as well. But it'll follow him wherever he goes," She said.

I've never been in the army or the Special Air Service, I thought to myself as I heard them finish their conversation. The distance between us grew as I walked my dog back home, and they were soon out of sight.

I had spent my school days looking out of the classroom window as I loved to get outdoors and explore. My dream job was to be a wildlife ranger with the Forestry Commission, but my career officer said I could get outdoor experience I'd wanted through a Youth Training Scheme, so I ended up on a Fleetwood golf course. After a 12-month stint there, I went back to the careers officer who had told me that because it actually was entirely different work. I felt gutted at that.

Now, I was 27, and home for me was a two-room flat on the seafront comprised of a front room come bedsit and a decent sized kitchen. I was on the dole. It was November 5, 1989, Bonfire Night, when all this began. I'd finished my walk with the dog, coming home to find Gary Jones and

Susan Moorcroft on the doorstep next door. I'd known Gary from my school days, and Susan was the sister of an old girlfriend of mine.

When I saw them, I thought back to when my best mate at school, Terry, said to me one summer afternoon as I sat in the front garden, "Don't look Danny Seabrook in the eyes as he can't stand up for himself." Danny was a classmate of Terry and me.

I had looked up at Terry but never replied to him. It was about a week later at school when he said to me, "You can look Danny Seabrook in the eyes now because he can stand up for himself."

Now, here as I eyed Gary and Susan, I heard Gary say something about me too low for me to hear, and Susan started laughing. I felt just like Danny Seabrook must have when he couldn't stand up for himself.

I opened the front door, went into my flat, and then punched the wardrobe in anger. I could hear my neighbors going back and forth about me smashing up my flat. I heard them come running around and enter the front door. Then I heard the lad from the upstairs flat say, "I wouldn't go down there if I was you. The lad used to spar with a boxer."

I sat down waiting for them to knock on my flat door, but no one did. It was sometime later that I went next door and rang the doorbell. When a lad answered, I asked him if Gary was in.

"Don't ask me," He remarked.

"You can tell him I don't punch people for fun," I said as I walked away.

The next day, I was out walking my dog along the seafront, just near the swimming baths, and there were two lads walking towards me. One of them was Jack who lived in one of the flats above me, but the other lad I didn't know.

"That's him." Jack pointed out.

I glanced at them but carried on walking not taking any notice.

"Show me where he lives, and I'll start it," said the other lad.

As soon as I arrived home, the minute I got back in, I could hear the neighbors saying they had put me on the street fighters list because I couldn't stand up for myself.

After that, I learned coughing was some kind of signal back then, and it was usually three or four coughs. It started when I went to the newsagents to pick up my magazine. A woman was standing to the side of me, and as I looked at the chap behind the counter, she stamped her feet and gave out three or four loud coughs. I turned to look at her, but she lowered her eyes towards the floor. I noticed after this that people stopped making eye contact with me.

"That's him." They would say, and when I looked to make eye contact with them, they would look towards the floor.

I would go into a shop and buy junk food, biscuits, or a pie, and someone would say, 'mustn't be SAS.' However, if I bought healthy food such as vegetables or pasta, then I would hear, 'must be SAS.' I was out every day with my dog, walking him near the Sea Cadet Base across the road from the Rossell picnic site, and in the parking lot, there was a large white van with dark bin bags to black out the windows. The neighbors next door to me said it was the SAS in the van. The SAS wanted me to snare hares and collect wild plants at night time on the golf course as part of my SAS training.

They were planning an assault course I had to do. I would sit in my flat at night time listening to them telling me what I should do.

There were several people next door watching me through infra-red cameras and listening to me through microphones in the wall. One was a psychiatrist who would visit me every night; he'd hypnotized me from next door convincing me to not stand up for myself, and he called me Knowles.

"Knowles, stay mesmerized," People would say to me followed by, "That's him."

One afternoon, I had an appointment at the dentist. The receptionist asked me my name and date of birth.

"Oh, I know that," A lady standing next to me said.

"How would you know that?" The receptionist asked.

",! Because I am his mother." She replied.

My mother had died when I was 4 years old. I remember the trips to the cemetery to visit her grave when I was young, but I remember nothing of my mother.

I was soon taken in to see the dentist, and I heard him make a comment to the dental nurse about my hand. I looked at my hand and could see that it was swollen. I'd thought back to the time I'd punched the wardrobe, but I said nothing. On the way out, I heard the dentist make a sexual comment about me, and the dental nurse started laughing.

"I bet he used to spar with a boxer too," Was his last remark.

As I made my way out of the dental office, I heard someone say the SAS were waiting in a car outside for me. When I made my way out of the exterior door, I glanced at a lad sitting in a Land Rover parked there, and he started the engine. Not giving any more attention to him, I made my way home.

I could hear people talking about me next door, saying things like I'd not had a shave or wash today or that I've not washed my clothes. This kept me on top of my household jobs. One day, I'd heard a remark that I'd not had a shower, so I took one. I couldn't understand while I was in the shower how I could still hear the people from next door talking to me.

I didn't have a TV license, and because I was on benefits, I couldn't afford one, so I just listened to radio Cumbria a lot or played my music. I would listen to the radio and hear the comments they would make about me. Every time I went out of my flat, either to the toilet or for a walk, my clock sitting on top of the gas fireplace would have changed to being too fast or too slow. Then I would turn on my radio to correct the time.

I could hear the SAS next door saying I'd had a box implanted in my head to give me supersonic hearing, and every time I was outside, I could hear voices and noises in the distance while chatting with people. I became very alert to my surroundings. I remember thinking to myself that there should be scars or some kind of marks on my head if they'd planted a box inside it, but I couldn't see them.

It soon became clear in my mind that the IRA were close and out to get me because the SAS wanted me to join them. People who sat in cars were SAS or the IRA.

I would sleep a lot in the weeks coming up to Christmas and began to notice that I'd fall asleep after drinking a cup of coffee.

"We've drugged his coffee," said my neighbors.

Then, as soon as I started drinking tea, they said my tea is drugged, so I started drinking water. They drugged the water too. I thought to myself, 'Who'd go to all that trouble to drug my water at the mains?'

"It's the psychiatrist," They said next door.

It then dawned on me that someone had easy access to my flat for all this to happen. I couldn't figure out who. The SAS, the IRA, the police. Who?

I was still walking my dog every day, and on one particular day, I was on the beach with some other dog walkers. I could see a police van on the lower walk and could just make out the PA system on the roof of the van. As I was walking along, I could hear the police in the van saying they could hear our conversation through the PA system in the van.

I did the best I knew how despite the voices. I spent time with my dog for comfort, and the two of us walked every day. With Christmas coming, I went to the pet shop to buy my dog a present. My State Benefits check hadn't arrived yet, but that didn't put me off buying a present for him. So off I went. They had some nice dog coats, so I decided on one and had to guess the size for him. When I was paying for it at the counter, a man standing there opened his wallet.

"I'll pay for that," He said.

"I am C.I. D, and we've got our eye on him, oh! And we've got his benefits check." He added.

I paid for the item, got my change, and walked out of the shop.

He followed and told me, "He's SAS as well, oh! He can't stand up for himself, but it'll follow him wherever he goes."

I went back sometime later and told them that the dog coat wouldn't fit my dog. They gave me my money back because they didn't have a bigger size for him. I also realized my benefits check still hadn't come through the post, and now it was already Christmas. I don't know when over Christmas it was, but I was soon eating dog biscuits and raw Brussel sprouts.

Then, one day I came out of my flat, walked down the street, and as I turned the corner, I heard someone say, "SAS man."

I glanced over my shoulder, and there in the middle of the road, was a man pointing a gun at me. 'What a prat,' I thought to myself.

Another afternoon, after my walk, I sensed there was something wrong. Someone had been in my flat.

"He knows," They said. "The C.I.D have been searching his flat."

I was so annoyed at this that I went around to the police station to complain and asked them why the Criminal Investigation Department had been searching my flat. The officer behind the desk went to check out my complaint. He came back and said the C.I.D hadn't been in my flat. It was on my way out that I looked over my shoulder, and I could see them laughing at me behind the reinforced panels.

My neighbors talked about me all the time, never stopping, and the only rest I got from their chat was when I slept. They watched me at night through the cameras on the wall.

One night, I fell asleep only to be woken up by someone ringing my doorbell. I could hear them banging and kicking the front door for someone to open it.

I could hear someone say, "Where is he? Show me where he lives! And I'll start it."

I heard the glass panel on the front door break, and then I could hear them go upstairs saying, "Where is he?"

When it had quietened down, I walked around to the police station to report it. I told them about the street fighters list and that someone was out to get me.

"Are they still in the building?" They inquired.

I answered yes. The officer replied that they'd send someone round to look at my flat, but I was more worried that they were after me. The officer also said I could use reasonable force to protect myself, and when I told him that the one after me was said to be a Karate expert, they agreed to send a van around. I never saw or heard the police van come.

There was a Mini car that I would see two or three times a day, flashing its brake lights and sounding its horn at me every time I saw it. As I walked to my aunt's house on Boxing Day, I saw the same Mini car following me again.

On the way to my aunt's, I stopped in at the Shell garage to buy a Mars bar, and as I was paying for it, I looked around for a clock to see what time it was. As I started to leave, the guy behind me took out what looked to be his checkbook.

The guy behind the till asked, "What's he looking for?"

"A clock." The man with the checkbook answered him.

"He doesn't know what time it is. SAS sign here, then we can go," He said.

I took no notice and walked out of the shop. I could hear him saying to the counter assistant that he was SAS, and they wanted me to join them. On my way out, I was thinking to myself, 'All this to make me stand up for myself; then they'll have a long wait. I am not having people telling me what to do or how I should live my life.'

"And he can't stand up for himself. We'll follow him wherever he goes." The man at the station said.

As I carried on my walk to my aunt's, I bumped into an old school friend, and we got to chatting. He was telling me how he'd applied to work on the oil rigs. I thought it strange that he remained in eye contact and never mentioned the SAS or that I couldn't stand up for myself. Everyone else seemed to mention that and look away. We chatted for about 20 minutes before I continued on my way.

While I was at my aunt's, my cousin, Rob, came around. I was sitting in the front room with my uncle, and Rob was in the kitchen with my aunt. I could hear him telling her not to make eye contact with me because I can't stand up for myself.

"Oh! That's silly." my aunt exclaimed.

He talked about Susan and how people in Fleetwood had made a collection for us. They would buy a cottage in the country. If I stand up for myself, then it would be ours. He'd said how they'd bought a camper van for us too. They parked the van on the road near the pitch and putt Golf course on the seafront. I'd talked to some dog walkers about the camper van and how it never seemed to move, always being parked in the same spot.

"Oh! I will tell him." My aunt said.

"No, Ma, he's not supposed to know. It'll follow him wherever he goes." Rob responded.

I left after hearing all that and walked back home. I saw the same Mini car again, flashing its brake lights and sounding its horn at me as I walked. I soon arrived home. I switched on the radio, and I could hear the neighbors again. They were telling me to kill myself with my kitchen knife, and then they would have my name. This would happen on various nights. I would get the urge to kill myself. To stop this urge, I would take my dog out at all hours.

One of my neighbors invited me around for a Christmas drink at his house. As he handed me a can of beer, I heard him say to me, "Here, this'll de-mesmerize you." I drank it; I am not a drinking man, but it tasted good.

It was a few days after my Christmas drink that I went to the pub, the bar on Fleetwood pier, one night to buy another beer. The bar seemed crowded, and I could hear everyone talking about me. People I met in there said how well I looked. This was too much for me so I walked back home.

I'd been getting this strange feeling in my legs – a weakness in my groin and legs – and I can only assume it was the lack of food. I could hear my neighbors saying I had an inbuilt compass in my legs that would point north, but I didn't like this feeling because it would also point me in the direction of the assault course they wanted me to do while I was out walking my dog.

After my neighbors started telling me to blacken my face with a burnt cork, I'd had enough and wanted to get away from them. I started walking and walked from Fleetwood to Cleveleys. As I got into Cleveleys, I could hear people making comments about me. I continued walking and ended up at St. Michael's on Wyre. I was thirsty and hungry, but I only had enough money to buy a can of Coke and a Mars bar, so I stopped into the petrol station there.

As I was paying for the can of Coke and Mars bar, the man in there said, "No, that's wrong." Then he went back to the till.

"That's all right. He can't add up anyway, and he's SAS too." The man standing next to me said.

I made my way out of the filling station, thinking to myself, 'It followed me all the way here.' I began to walk back home. It was then that I realized I'd left my dog at home. I was in tears on my journey back. It was getting dark, and I was a long way from home. All told, I walked 26 miles that day having no idea it was that far. As I was coming up to the roundabout near Skipool Creek, a taxi pulled up in front of me, and out popped Susan. I heard her say, 'John!', but I couldn't quite hear the rest of what she said. Then she jumped back in the taxi and was gone in a flash.

I continued my journey back home, and under every bush and tree I came across, I could hear the SAS making comments about me. When I got back to Fleetwood, people were saying how they would report me to the

RSPCA for leaving my dog at home. At home, I turned my radio up loud to drown out the voices. The SAS were in the garden ready to storm my flat. They were armed and had stun grenades. I could hear them whispering outside my flat.

That's when it dawned on me. Something was wrong because I could still hear my neighbors next door over my radio. I knew this wasn't right.

I burst into tears. My world had come crashing down around me. I knew there was something more to this. There was no way on earth that I should be able to hear my neighbors talking about me over a radio blasting out loud music. I could only do one thing and that was to walk to my Aunt Betty's for help. She was chatting to her friend, and when her friend had left, she called my aunt Cath. I was still in tears when my aunt Cath arrived. The two of them took me to see my GP.

I can remember sitting in the waiting room to see my doctor, a General Practitioner, and while there, I could hear one lad saying how I was SAS and also how I couldn't stand up for myself. I must have had priority to see my GP because I was called next. She asked me if I'd heard voices, and I answered yes. She pointed me toward a compact room having both my aunts follow us in there.

"You can wait in here until the ambulance comes."

While in there, I heard the lad from the waiting room talking to my GP.

"Where is he?" He wanted to know.

"Who?" Replied my GP.

"The lad who can't stand up for himself. Is he in here?" He asked.

"No! You can't go in there." I heard my GP say.

"If he's in there, tell him I'll start it. It'll follow him wherever he goes." He stated.

It went all quiet as I stood there waiting for him to open the door. After what seemed like an eternity of silence, my GP opened the door and directed me to an awaiting ambulance that had pulled up outside. As I got into the ambulance, I gave my aunt my flat keys, so she could look after my dog for me. Away I went to the hospital.

Chapter 2

Voluntary Admission to Parkwood

When the ambulance pulled up outside the psychiatric unit, they took me up to a ward where I had to see the nurse. She asked me a series of questions like name, date of birth, am I on any medication, do I take drugs, and am I hearing voices. I then waited to see a consultant, and it was sometime later when he came to see me. They took me into a small room and asked more questions. Do you know where you are? Why do you think you are here? After the consultation with him, I heard him say to one nurse.

"Just keep him in for a few days, and then let him go."

They showed me to a bed, which I had to make up myself, for the night. The nurse returned with some bedding which she handed me to make up my bed.

Here, I met a patient called David because he was just standing beside me as I made up my bed. I got no response to any of my questions I asked him. David followed me every day while I was in there.

When the nurse came back, she told David he shouldn't be in here as he's on another ward. He looked at me and walked away without saying a word. The nurse handed me a pill, a glass of water and some PJs. I took my pill and handed her the glass back. Then she left me by my bed. I had no idea what time it was. I knew it was just after New Year 1990 but not what time it was. I went looking for a clock and wandered into the dayroom. The TV was on. I heard a report on Granada Television. I didn't look at the TV, but someone had remarked it was me on the local news. I sat down for an hour or two listening to the patients on the ward and my own voices.

Everywhere I went in the hospital, they were talking about me. I tried to get away from it by listening to the hospital radio by my bed, but I couldn't distract myself from what they were saying. The only relief I got from the voices was when I was sleeping, so off I went to bed. I went to the toilet in the night and collapsed on the floor. I got myself up and sat on the toilet. I sat there for some minutes, I had a wee and went back to bed, but I told no one about it.

The first weeks in the hospital, I wasn't allowed to go off the ward, and I had to have my meals in the dayroom. After mealtimes came the long queues for medication time. I remember when I took my meds, one doctor would put our meds in his hand. Then he would hand them to us while other doctors would use a plastic cup.

It was later that this same doctor would say, "Oh! No arsenic."

When he handed me my medication, I didn't react, but from there on he would always say, "arsenic" whenever he handed me my meds.

I can't remember which night it was, but it was around 3 am when the fire alarms went off. My reaction was so quick that I was up and dressed before the nurse could tell me they were testing the alarms. Even at visiting times, if I would be on my bed sleeping and my relatives would arrive, I was up and alert before they could sit down by my bed. Visiting time was always busy with relatives and friends coming to see patients. This made it hard to find somewhere quiet to speak with your visitors. Everyone was talking about me and not making eye contact with me.

"This's him." "That's him." "He's SAS as well." They would say amongst other things.

I'd taken nothing with me when I went into hospital. One nurse approached me to tell me I needed a shave, but I told him I haven't anything to shave with, so he said he could lend me a razor. I borrowed some shaving foam from one of the patients. When it came time for me to have a bath, I went to the office to borrow some bubble bath. They just started laughing at me, but as usual, I said nothing.

I was having injections of Dipixol, though I wasn't keen on needles, and I asked why I need to have it.

"To slow you down." Was the nurse's reply.

I could see the plants stalking me from across the day room. I heard one patient make a comment that he could see them stalking him too.

I was on a high dose of Largactil, an antipsychotic medication, along with Procyclidine to combat the side effects of the Largactil.

There were a number of people who seemed to collapse for no reason. One chap that I used to chat with every day had his arm in a cast, and when I asked him why he was in here, he pointed to his cast saying he'd broken his arm. 'But this is a psychiatric hospital,' I thought to myself. One morning I couldn't see him in the dayroom, and I went looking for him. I found him in his bed. He said he felt weak and collapsed on the ward. I don't know why, but over the next few days, I would sit by his bed and chat with him.

I would often sit in the quiet room by myself and watch the rabbits come out at nightfall. It was my salvation, the closest I could get to the outdoors and nature.

I mentioned to my consultant when I'd had my initial consultation with him that I have schizophrenia, and he said to me, 'it's too early to tell.'

I'd had a weird experience in my body. I was sitting in the dayroom; I could feel what felt like static electricity coming from the floor, traveling up my legs to build up in my body. Then, I would feel a spasm of an electric type shock, or shudder, through my whole body. Then it would start all over again.

I put my feet up on a table (electricity can't travel through wood, or at least I thought so). But this didn't work so off I went to lie on my bed. This seemed to ease it for a while only for it to come back after a bit. On the ward, they were saying it's ECT (electro-convulsive therapy) for my illness from the psychiatrist. 'That's impossible,' I thought to myself.

I would sit in the dayroom watching the patients. I could always guarantee that two patients who were chatting to each other would say "let's make love"; then they'd walk off somewhere together. I heard this for the first time when I was sitting with my aunties during a visiting time. One of the lady patients sat down next to us, looked at me, and offered, "Let's make love."

I sat there feeling embarrassed as I looked at her for a few minutes. Then she got up and walked away. I heard one of my aunts ask, 'what did she say?' 'Let's make love' my other aunt replied.

Other family visited me too. I'd not seen my dad for some years, however, he came to visit me in the hospital with my sister, Louise. I heard him say 'sorry' as he shook my hand. Sorry! I thought to myself. Why? I was the one who was ill, and soon I'll be back on my feet; I know I can get through this.

A nurse approached me one day to take my blood for lab work and took me into a treatment room. I wasn't keen to have it done, as like with my injections, I didn't like needles. It had to be done though.

"Sharp scratch. Oh! But your SAS," He said.

Then, as I came out of the treatment room, I'd heard someone say I'd just had a blood test for HIV.

In my head, I couldn't reason with what people were saying, and I wouldn't let them get to me either. I also knew when I got better that what was left would be reality, not my illness.

Tom, my brother, came to see me with Louise and surprised me by bringing Toby, my dog. They took me for a walk around the local nature reserve with my dog, but I wasn't one bit keen on this. People were saying, "He's SAS" or "That's him." They were waiting for me to make my escape over the fields.

It was difficult to make out what was fact from reality and to reason with what people were saying. This just made my illness worse. I suffered with what people were saying but not knowing if it was reality.

When they allowed me to go to the canteen for my meals, I found this was an even longer queue to get a meal. The hardest thing about psychiatric hospitals is the queues. Like everything else, I'd endure this too. Even though it wasn't time for my meds, they had us wait in the queue for medication four times a day.

We had to do our own washing and ironing on the wards too. I went to the office to ask them to show me how to iron my clothes so one nurse took me to the laundry room to show me how to do this.

I'd heard him say to me, "What? You can't do your own ironing? You've been in the army." As usual, I didn't reply.

Just before one visiting time, David followed me to my room, and I sat in my chair next to my bed. David laid down on my bed, arms behind his head and, as usual, never said a word. I tried to get a conversation out of him, but no luck so I left him there stretched out on my bed. I couldn't help but keep wondering what was going through his mind. I didn't see him as a threat to me, and I don't know why he chose to follow me.

When I could leave the hospital for short outings, I went to the shops with a patient called Glenda. She took me by bus, and once as we stood waiting at the bus stop, all of a sudden, she kissed me on the lips. I was gobsmacked by this. I was still hearing voices. I wondered what this poor girl must have been going through to kiss a total stranger. We got on the bus and soon arrived at the shops. I could hear her saying all kinds of things to me about how I was her boyfriend now.

She took me into a little coffee shop and asked me if I'd like to buy her a coffee. But I didn't have any money, and I told her so. With that, she got up and walked out of the coffee shop leaving me sitting there by myself. I ended up walking the mile and a half back to the hospital by myself.

I began OT work (Occupational Therapy), and I'd decided on music, pottery, and cooking. I liked the cooking, and I'd get to walk into Blackpool to buy the items on my shopping list. The OT workers soon found I was walking into Blackpool instead of using the bus, and they continued to allow me to walk there and back because I couldn't use public transport by myself.

The meals we cooked were for 4 or 5 people, and as we cooked them at lunchtimes, they told us we could eat what we had cooked. However, we couldn't take leftover food onto the ward so what we had left we put in the garbage bin. I thought this was a waste of our food and money.

Music sessions were just patients sitting around a large stereo playing music of our choice and then discussing what we'd played. I like music. When people made comments about me all the time, I would get annoyed and just get up and walk out of the group a few times.

In pottery class, we all sat at a table chatting and experimenting with a lump of clay to see what came out of it. That's what they told me to do, and I ended up making an ashtray which pleased me. I wasn't able to take it home with me though as it exploded in the kiln. This made me sad even though I didn't smoke.

Next, I made a swan that survived the kiln. It was my Aunt Betty who wanted to buy it from the hospital for about 50 pence. The payment was for the weight of the clay, and it went back into the hospital funds. When Aunt Betty and I wandered down to the pottery room during visiting time, we couldn't find it. Someone else must have bought it.

Now that I could go out of the hospital by myself, I would walk almost every day into Blackpool town center, taking a route through the park opposite the hospital and then into town. I did it for exercise as I am used to walking every day. I didn't like being cooped up in the hospital all the time.

One of the OT workers said she wanted to see me, to see how I was getting on with my OT work. Part of my sessions involved joining in a parachute game and a ball game which I didn't like one bit. To me, these games are for 8-year-olds and not for adults in a psychiatric hospital. When I told her that, she said she'd put me in this new group which they'd just formed for people who don't like groups. How comical, I thought as I laughed to myself.

In this group, we played a game where a famous person's name written on a sticky label was stuck on our foreheads. Then we'd take turns asking questions about this famous person as we'd try to guess who it was. This was just as bad as the parachute game as not only was it childish, but it also made us feel ridiculous.

On one of my walks, on my way back to the hospital, I saw a woman had collapsed in the park. As I turned and walked towards her, this guy shouted out, "It's ok", so I changed direction to continue on back to the hospital. Then another guy approached her, and I heard him say, "It's all right, he can't stand up for himself. He's SAS as well."

I ignored him and walked back to Parkwood Hospital. I could see one guy phoning for an ambulance. Someone was taking care of it after all and didn't need my help.

They allowed me to go home for my first weekend away from the hospital. My dad and step mum took me home. When I got home, they came into my flat for a while, and when they'd left, there was complete silence. It was a stark contrast to the continual noise of the hospital. I sat there for a few hours with my dog, and that's when it hit me: there were no voices from next door. I cried that weekend. I couldn't believe what I'd been through, and it had taken its toll on me. It was all beginning to sink in.

When I got back to the hospital on that Sunday, I told the consultant that I'd cried most of the weekend. I can't remember his exact words, but he said that my weekends home would be stopped for a few weeks. I walked out on the consultant back to the ward.

My voices had lessened now. The voices I had at home were gone. No more telling me I should have a wash, bath, shave or to wash my clothes, and keeping on top of this had become difficult. What's left would be what people were saying? All they would ever talk about was the SAS.

"That's him", "This is him", "It'll follow him wherever he goes" to name a few things they were saying.

When I was by myself, I was fine, but whenever I came across people, they looked to the ground in disgust towards me.

"That's him." They would say, trying to get a response from me, but I'd head to the quiet room and sit in there or anywhere else it was quiet. When it got overbearing for me, usually around 10 pm, I would head off to the park or the golf course in the pitch blackness to be by myself. I would always sit by myself in the canteen and gaze out of the window, looking at the rabbits opposite me on the golf course.

Because I was so unwell, and in the hospital, it was easy to keep on top of my hygiene. Everything was done for me, including tablets and meals, and there are not as many daily stresses in there as I would discover over the years after I left.

They introduced me to two guys from the Wyre Community Support Team, Andrew, a Social Worker, and Gary, a CPN (Community Psychiatric Nurse). As I entered the room they were in, I heard one of them say, "That's him."

I smiled as the other one looked to the ground.

"And he can't stand up for himself." I heard one say.

When this had started, it caused me to stop making eye contact with people. What was the point if all people ever do is to look to the ground whenever I try to make eye contact with them? I shook their hands, and I knew I was getting ready for a discharge in time.

I thought, If I am well enough for discharge, then I must be on the way to recovery. But why then are people saying what they're saying, and why are they refusing to make eye contact with me?

I put this question to my consultant's assistant psychiatrist.

"Why do people refuse to make eye contact with me?" I asked him.

"Do you know I've noticed that too?" He replied.

I didn't respond to him, and all I could come up with is that if this is not because of my illness, then what remains is my reality. All he said was that my meds need to be increased. I told him I didn't feel too well because my meds were dropped all of a sudden.

"Yes! They've dropped by almost a half all of a sudden when they shouldn't have been." He said after checking my doses.

Another mental escape I found was to sit on a bench in the sun. This was another quiet spot for me as it overlooked the golf course. Well, a nurse said to me he'd seen me sitting in the sun every day. He warned me about the dangers of turning pink in the sun because of my high dose of Largactil. It was the same nurse who told me the injections of Dipixol were to slow me down.

I'll never know whether the nurse was taking the micky out of me or not. I know it was his actual voice and not one in my head.

Being able to spend weekends at home was getting me ready for a discharge. My dad would take me out for a walk and a coffee, and we went to places like Lytham St. Anne's along with my step mum. We also went to Glasson Dock to where I bought the coffee, and I would hear her say things like. "Watch it, John." She always said it when anyone would say something like "That's him", and then they'll say the usual after that like "It'll follow him wherever he goes. Oh! He's SAS too" or "Oh! But he's not a bad lad, really."

I couldn't respond to this because it was always delayed when I picked up on it. So, by the time I'd heard it some time had gone by. I put the delay down to the psychiatrist who'd hypnotized me somehow without me knowing. All I could do is to suffer this and just walk away from it.

A week before my discharge was due, I was in pottery class, and David was sitting next to me. Then all of a sudden, he stood up, shook my hand, and said, "Well done."

With that, he walked out of the pottery class. I asked the OT worker what was all that about.

"I don't know." She replied.

I was puzzled at this because I told no one I was being discharged yet.

My discharge had come around, and I was going home. On my last day, my dad was coming to pick me up and take me home, otherwise, it would have been in the back of an ambulance. However, he was late, and I was getting agitated at this, so I rang Louise to see where he was because it wasn't like him to be so late. I started looking out of the windows to see if I could see him coming. I was so eager to get out of there and be back home again.

When he arrived, I already had my belongings in plastic carrier bags, so I gathered them along with my medication and away we went home.

I'd spent a full 9 weeks in the psychiatric hospital, and now, I was glad to get out of there. The first thing I wanted to do was to dispose of that kitchen knife. To take it round to the police station because that had to go.

They discharged me to the Support Team and a support worker named Amanda. I sat in my flat wondering what the future would hold for me, if any. What would my life be like now?

I still had my dog, and thankfully the RSPCA hadn't taken him away from me. However, people were still saying "This's him", "That's him", "It'll follow him wherever he goes" amongst other things. The fact was they were still saying I am SAS when I wasn't, and they wouldn't make eye contact with me but instead still look at the ground.

I'd been to hell and back, so now it was time to get back on my feet and begin this journey to recovery.

Chapter 3

My Childhood and Onward

Growing up with no mother wasn't easy, and when I went to Terry's house, I'd always envy him as he had a mum. A mum is your mum and your best friend too. She's there to give you kisses when you fall or hurt yourself, but for me, I guess my two elder sisters took that role.

My dad must have had it hard bringing up five kids. He worked as a lumper on Fleetwood docks unloading the fish that came in on the boats. I can still remember the fish he brought home, Haddock and Cod, and Cod Roe too. I loved the Cod Roe he brought home. I would first boil it and then fry it and eat it on a sandwich.

We never had pocket money, but our holidays made up for that. My dad loved Scotland, and it became our love too. We would visit Edinburgh Castle almost every year to see the Military Tattoo held there. My dad was an ex-military, and he loved the Edinburgh Military Tattoo as they hold a spectacular display there. Many a time, we parked overnight in a wayside stop, and we would watch the deer and rabbits in the surrounding countryside.

I can remember that I could hear things being said about me in my childhood. One summer day, I was having my tea, and I heard my dad say to me, "John, you're sweating like a bloody fat pig."

I wasn't looking at him, but I know it was in his voice. I would always hear someone say something in my childhood, and all I knew was it was in their voice.

At school, they said I was shy, but even then, I was a loner, and much preferred being on my own. The more people I am around the quieter I become; I like wide open spaces.

When I was in primary school, Mr. Nook, our teacher, took us to Beacon Fell on a school trip. I was fascinated by the squirrels there and wanted to wander off by myself to track them.

I learned about the sycamore, oak, and maple trees. The seeds of sycamore and maple are like helicopters, and when you throw them up into the air, they come spiraling down to the ground. Horse chestnut and the sweet chestnut are other trees I learned about too. We would gather the horse chestnuts and soak them in vinegar, bake them in the oven, and use them to play conkers at school.

In my secondary school, one day I was on the playground, and I got into a fight with another school kid. I'd heard Terry say to me, "Fuckin' batter him."

The fight had to be broken up by one teacher. I'd gotten a cut lip from the whole experience.

I'd be first in class to get a desk near the windows, so I could sit looking out. I wanted to be outside exploring in the fresh air no matter what the weather. As for football and sport, I hated that, but I still had to do it. I also didn't like the long distance running either, despite being the second fastest runner in my junior school.

We played on the mountains, in the fields and streams because we all loved the outdoors. I knew the outdoors was for me, and that's where I wanted to be, out in the hills and fields amongst nature.

I developed an interest in tracking and survival skills. I also liked wild food, herbal teas, and coffees. When I got a flat by myself, I would often gather Nettles, Elder flowers,

Ladies Fingers and Beech Nuts, Cleavers Bramble root for herbal teas and coffees. I made cakes with Blackberries, Blackberry and Apple pie, and Nettle quiche. I would often carry a haversack wherever I went to collect them.

We went fishing up the Scotland and Cumbria coast, and I would often go fishing at night. We picked Cockles off the Fleetwood beach, went shrimping, and dug our own worms for fishing. I always felt comfortable outdoors even when I was by myself. It wasn't like today with children stuck on their computers.

My first job was on the golf course at Fleetwood as a trainee greenskeeper. I remember looking north at cottages in Scotland for sale at £1,000 in the Exchange and Mart. That's not a lot of money today, but on my wage of £19 a week, it was well out of my price range. I think to myself now, if I'd gone for one of those cottages, maybe my life would be different, however, I know now you can't alter the past and that everything happens for a reason.

After my 12 months as a trainee greenskeeper, I went back on benefits and was looking for another job. I also spent my time on local wasteland, and I'd often walk along the disused railway line to Stanah Country Park. There was a lovely view of the Forest of Bowland. I would sit and look across the river before walking on to Skippool Creek. This is a nice area along the river and near to Poulton. I soon began walking on from Skipool Creek and over Shard Bridge, and from here, I'd begun to explore Over Wyre.

I started work at Frank Richmond Limited, a fencing manufacturer, where I made overlap fencing panels, concrete posts, and concrete base panels. It was only a five-minute walk from the wasteland I played on as a kid. I would often sit on an old air raid shelter there and take in everything around me. I loved sitting there watching the rabbits and listening to the birds.

I must have worked here for around 15 months when I had a disagreement with the boss, and he fired me. Soon after, he asked me to come back, and I declined to do so, maybe because I am an excellent worker or the fact that I was right.

I was back at the dole queue and signing on every fortnight, which I hated. I went to live with my sister, Louise, and her full house of 4 adults and 3 children. It was a while before I had another job, this time at Lexmain Limited. It was shift work of 8-hour shifts. I was packing plastic bags into cardboard boxes. They based it in Poulton which was miles away, but walking to work and back never bothered me at all.

The job didn't suit me as I wanted to be outdoors and working in the countryside. I wrote many letters to the Forestry Commission seeking work with them. Sometimes I got replies, and sometimes I didn't. I even wrote to them saying I'd offer my services for free, however, they wrote back to say their insurance wouldn't cover me. My dream job was a wildlife ranger for the Forestry Commission.

I moved out from my sister's place to live with my Aunt Cath. While I was living there, I'd taken out a loan for a motorbike to get to my job and back, and I now had wheels to travel further afield to places like the Forest of Bowland, the likes of Scorton Picnic Site, and Brock. I loved to get out and explore them.

Since starting work at Frank Richmond Limited, I'd not been fishing as much as I used to, maybe because I was looking for work or was actually working. I was still getting outdoors though, and I was still trying to practice some tracking skills, even in a town, like the signs of the postman leaving his rubber bands on the pavement. Today, I am not an excellent tracker, and I recognize if my illness hadn't taken away 20 years of my life, I'd have more skills now.

There's no saying when my schizophrenia began to take over my life. It could have been in my 20s or even earlier. I can remember staying at my Aunt Cath's but not why I said to her I may as well commit suicide before going off on my motorbike. My aunt got worried as she phoned the police. I didn't go home that night either but went straight to work. A police officer came to my place of work looking for me and took me outside for a chat. I can remember him saying to me, "The next time you want to commit suicide just do it and don't get us involved."

I guess in my childhood there were signs of me hearing voices, but the cause was unknown. I'm not sure whether the death of my mother at such a young age had anything to do with it. My Aunt Cath said I would shadow my mum, following her around all the time. At such a young age, I don't hold any memories of my mum, and I always wish I could turn back the clock. Life still waits for no man though.

Here I was working shifts and not sleeping much either, maybe from the stress of the job. I wasn't there long when they laid me off, but before I could sign back up for benefits, they rehired me. This time my shifts were 12 hours. Even with these long shifts, my sleep patterns didn't change, and I was sleeping only 3 or 4 hours over a 24-hour period. When I think about my life and the jobs I've had, I never seemed to sleep much when in committed work.

The company that I was working for must have been having problems. I was laid off yet again and back signing on the dole. My next job was at a nightclub in Blackpool as a cloakroom attendant for only five hours a night, four nights a week. I worked here for about a year until one night I turned up to work, and they fired me on the spot. This never bothered me as I just walked away from them. It was sometime later after signing back on that I found out they'd told the benefits people I swore in front of two managers.

I moved out of my aunt's place and into a flat on the seafront. I'd started fishing again, and I was living on my own for the first time in my life. I was lucky to get the flat as I was still on benefits but my landlady had known one of my uncles at school.

Here, I was still trying for a job that suited me in the outdoors, and at one point, I traveled to Scotland by train for a keeper's job in a forest. When they interviewed me, it surprised me that they offered me a job there. One of the conditions for the job was that I'd have to work the first 6 months on benefits, if the Department of Work and Pensions would allow it. Other conditions were if I wanted to go home for the weekend, I could, but if not, I'd have to work. Also, the wage they were offering was only £30 a week. They said Andrew, one of their employees, has been working here for 4 years, so he's getting £40 a week. I declined the job offer as I was getting more money on benefits, and the hours I'd have to work for that money wasn't enough.

I went out walking every day from my home to Poulton and Over Wyre too. I also walked on the wasteland where I played as a kid. It was here that I found Toby, my dog. He became my traveling companion for many years, and we walked miles together. I'd borrow my sister's car and take him to the Lake District and the Forest of Bowland in Lancashire.

I made friends with a guy called Thomas that I'd often see when I went fishing, and as I got to know him more, he told me he had been in a psychiatric hospital with paranoid schizophrenia. He was a great guy, and it was when I told him about a psychiatrist that came to see me at my flat, he said that's good as they can sort you out.

The psychiatrist said I should go to the day hospital in Blackpool, which I did. I got the tram into Blackpool seafront and walked through the town to the hospital. I still can't remember much about that day, but I know I talked to a nurse there. She said I had anxiety and anthropophobia which I couldn't make sense of at all. I am a loner, but I don't have a fear of people, so we agreed that I should attend the day hospital the following week.

As I was walking my dog on the beach one day, I saw Thomas digging bait. I went to chat with him, and he was holding his chest, complaining of chest pains. He went to the doctor the next day about it and then went home to get some rest. After I walked my dog, I went back out to dig some worms for him. I dug around 40 worms for him, wrapped them in newspaper, and went around to his home. When I knocked on the door, his mum answered, and when I asked for Thomas, she told me he'd passed away after complaining of chest pains. He'd had a heart attack.

He'd gone home and sat in his chair, and they found him lying on the floor dead. If only, I thought to myself. I should have gone home with him. He would still be alive if I'd done this, if I'd done that. I went back home and cried. I didn't go back to the hospital after that, and I remember them sending me a letter, but I ignored it. One must learn that you can't turn back the clock and must live with your past mistakes, however hurtful they are.

I attended Thomas's funeral, and it was a sad occasion for me. I can still picture Thomas on the beach complaining of chest pains, clutching his chest. It was after Thomas's death that I stopped fishing altogether. I did keep my fishing gear because I still might get that urge to go fishing once again.

Before Thomas's death, I'd talked to him about my struggles to get the work I liked, outdoor work. He mentioned that his relatives had a farm in Scotland. He could get me a job on this farm, but I declined the offer. I didn't want that kind of outdoor work. I miss Thomas today and still think of that day on the beach.

I was discussing with one of the Job Centre staff about what the hospital had said about me having a fear of people. She said that the psychiatrist could hypnotize me so I could work alongside people. They just could not understand me when I told them it wasn't a fear but more that I am a loner. They asked for a note from my doctor saying I had a phobia and anxiety, which I got them. It was not until some years later that I had the more severe diagnosis of paranoid schizophrenia.

It wasn't long after that, I started getting headaches. I ended up back at my doctor's again as I'd taken a whole packet of paracetamol, a pain killer, but to no avail. I told her that it was dangerous to take as many as I'd taken, and she agreed. I'd been given some capsules to take, which I did, but I stopped taking them as they weren't working.

Chapter 4

Recovery

Having spent nine weeks in a psychiatric hospital, they discharged me into the community. A community which doesn't understand mental illness let alone schizophrenia.

You see headlines in newspapers, and on television 'Man Stabbed in Street by Schizophrenic'. That's the impression most people have of schizophrenia and mental health. I now have a label which will follow me wherever I go, along with what people were saying about me.

"That's him."

"This is him."

"It'll follow him wherever he goes."

"He's SAS."

"The SAS will be waiting in a car outside for him."

I wasn't left to cope by myself in the community as I was under the local Mental Health team (Wyre Community Support Team). They soon introduced me to a support worker, Amanda. I remember this well when they first came around to visit me at my flat. I made them both a brew, and as I stood there in the kitchen's doorway listening to them talking, I heard:

"He's showing off." From my social worker.

I looked at them and said nothing to either of them. I just made them their brew.

The support team was comprised of a community psychiatric nurse (CPN), support workers, and social workers. My CPN would come around to give me my injection of Dipixol every two weeks. My first prescription of Dipixol came in pre-filled syringes complete with the needles, and they couldn't have had much trust in me because these were taken from me by my CPN. This was yet again an air of precaution by the mental health services. What they thought I'd do with them God knows because not all people with psychosis react in the same way.

Every Saturday, I'd walk with my dog Toby to my Dad's for dinner. We would sit around the table to eat. I'd listen to my Dad, Step Mum, and Stepsister talking about me. I'd just ignore them because if I said anything, I knew full well they'd deny it. Then I'd walk back home along the seafront, and still the people wouldn't make eye contact with me.

Amanda took me to the Discovery Centre at Garstang with another support worker, Diane. This was because I'd tried to join the Ranger Service, not to mention the Forestry Commission, when I was younger. When we arrived there and had a look around, Diane went up to the desk at the reception area to chat with one of the Rangers.

"Don't look him in the eye over there because he can't stand up for himself, and he wants to join the Ranger Service too."

"Oh, he's SAS as well."

As I looked at them, I could see the Ranger glance over to me, and I didn't say a word to them. No doubt, if I had said something, every time I heard them say something, they'd try to detain me against my will under the Mental Health Act.

There was another time when Amanda, Diane, another service user, and I went to the Lake District for a walk and went into a café there. We had all ordered our coffee and something to eat when Diane got up and walked back to the counter. Once more, I heard her say not to look me in the eye and that I couldn't stand up for myself, not to mention that I was SAS.

It was when Amanda moved to live in York that Diane became my support worker, and in all the time that I'd known her, Diane didn't look me in the eyes.

Since seeing my dad when he visited me in the hospital, I never once heard him say I couldn't stand up for myself or that I was SAS.

When my dad was with me, I could hear him say, "Watch it, John" when other people would make comments about me.

I asked my support team about my diagnosis of psychosis and whether I was schizophrenic, and they just said it covers a number of different illnesses. It was some years later when I went to get a sick note and they asked me what my diagnosis was that I said schizophrenia. From there on, my diagnosis was that of schizophrenia.

I also told my support team about me ending it all and my thoughts and voices from next door wanting me to commit suicide. I'd been through a lot with my illness, even breaking down in tears, and to me, suicide was the easy option.

My CPN who administered my injections of Dipixol every two weeks wouldn't make eye contact with me either. He always was nagging at me to get a color television. He even offered to take me into Blackpool to get one, but I would always decline his offer.

The support team had put me on a waiting list for a council flat. Maybe it was because of the condition of the flats I was living in. The council had soon found me somewhere else to live, and while I was reluctant to move, I still did. It was my dad, Louise, my sister, and my brother, Tom, who helped me move into the Fisherman's Cottages on Bloomfield Road in Fleetwood.

Diane mentioned a place called Making Space, a charity for mental health, that had spaces for an outward-bound course in the Lake District. She was pushing me to go on one of their adventure outings that they run every year. However, with people saying that I was SAS, I declined to go on them.

I was sleeping a lot during the day, and taking my dog out for walks through the night. Even with my dog beside me, I would still see the foxes in my local park under the street lighting as that's when they're more active. These walks were due to the timing of my medication. I always took my tablets on time, and I mentioned to my consultant the next time I saw him I was sleeping in the day and not at night. He juggled the dosage and the times I took them which seemed to work well in allowing me to sleep at night.

Another adventure they asked me about was yet again with Making Space. They had a hotel in Kendal which was run by service users. Yet again, I refused to go even though my support worker offered to go with me.

It was around this time I was thinking of getting a car and mentioned it to my CPN. He told me I need to inform the Driving and Vehicle Licensing Agency (DVLA) that I'd been in a psychiatric hospital. I did, and as luck would have it, they said I could still drive. I bought a red Metro hatchback car.

After coming out of the hospital, I'd stopped most my hobbies and interests except being outdoors. I still had a love for the outdoors, and now my car could get my dog and me to Stanah, Skippool Creek and the Forest of Bowland, all the places I used to walk with Toby before I became ill.

My diet had transformed. I'd started eating junk food and ready meals for convenience, apart from going around to my Dad's or Aunt's for a meal. I started eating chocolate and lots of it. Now, to get more fit and shed some weight, I'd started exercising more, and joined the local gym. I also changed my whole diet – no more chocolate for me – and I wanted to get back outdoors again.

Within the first week of joining the gym, I could hear people saying I was SAS. After my sessions at the gym, they would say that the SAS were waiting in a car outside for me. I'd be on my way out, and there would be someone sitting in a car outside. They'd start the car engine as I stepped outside.

I realized something was wrong, that I was relapsing, and I told my support team about it. I'd told no one about me signing up at the gym or my plans to get back to the outdoors. I was soon back to see a consultant, and because I'd changed my lifestyle, the Largactil wasn't working like it should be.

I was back in Parkwood Psychiatric Hospital for a change of tablets, and I spent 4 weeks in there once again. I was thinking long and hard whether my interests and hobbies were my illness. I like bushcraft and tracking not to mention the outdoors. I'd developed these interests at school. After a while, I came up with a theory. If a person goes to church and then develops schizophrenia, and if he hears voices saying that they are Jesus, should he stop going to church because of this? Well, the answer is no.

I asked my support team the same question, and they gave me the same answer. Why should I give up my hobbies and interests just because of my illness? I don't like football, cricket, or golf, nor do I drink, smoke, or take drugs? The only drugs I take are prescription medication from the doctors, so why should I let my illness dictate my life?

Schizophrenia took away much of my life, and now I wanted my life back. So, I started reading up about mental illness and came across a book called Welcome Silence by Carol North, which I found in my local library. This book inspired me so much. It's about a woman who has schizophrenia and her battle with it. I vowed to change my life for the better.

I had another support worker, Greg, who took me to a café in Carnforth when we went to look at a bookshop there. As we sat at a table in the café, I looked around and made eye contact with these two men.

"That's him," One guy said to the other.

"Don't look him in the eyes because he can't stand up for himself."

"Oh, he's SAS too."

I glanced back at them, and they both stopped making eye contact with me. I said nothing to my support worker, and we drank our coffee and left. I was in two minds how they would know me: we'd driven a long way from Fleetwood to Carnforth, and these were two total strangers to me. Yet I knew what I'd seen and heard.

Another time I was sitting in Greg's car, I'd ripped my pocket, and it needed sewing up. When he said he knew of a sewing group I could join, I declined to go.

"They learn to sew in the army," He said.

'What's the army got to do with this conversation?' I thought to myself, but I never replied to his comment.

It was when I was in my early 20s that I went to sign up for the Territorial Army, and from there, I wanted to join the Territorial SAS. I'd told no one my plans to do so when I'd gone for recruitment at the TA Barracks in Blackpool to sign up for the TA.

When I was due for the selection weekend for the TA, I wasn't keen on how the regulars treated the part-timers. I heard stories of the regulars throwing stones at the TA. That wasn't my style, so I didn't go, but I had told no one, not even my relations of my plans. I thought it could explain where some of my voices were coming from, but the question to me was how would they know it. I knew I had paranoia, but to me that paranoia was real.

One morning as I was coming out of my flat, I bumped into my stepsister. She'd stopped over to tell me my Dad was ill, and they'd called out an ambulance for him. She was on her way to work. I couldn't make out if she was trying to make me stand up for myself or what I was hearing were, in fact, voices.

It wasn't until sometime later that day, my Uncle Bob came around to tell me my Dad had passed away. I felt nothing, maybe because of my medication or my illness. I just had no feelings. He asked if I wanted to go to the funeral and offered to take me, so I said yes. He said he'd come and pick me up to take me there and back.

On the day of my Dad's funeral, I took my dog out for a walk and missed his funeral. I was too ill to go; I couldn't face people not making eye contact with me or what they might say. Not saying farewell to my dad turned out to be the biggest regret of my life. If I could turn back the clock, it would be to that day, to say my farewell and pay my last respects to him.

My support team had told me of a place called Clubhouse which had opened up in a portacabin on an old parking lot in town. It was for service users and run by two members of staff. They had activities and groups and helped people find jobs or volunteer work. I'd said no to lots of things they'd offered me over the years, but this time I'd thought I'd give it a go.

I can remember well when I went, they made me a cup of coffee, and I sat down by myself to drink it. I got up to go to the toilet, and it turned out to be the girl's toilets by mistake, so I went to sit back in my seat. The Clubhouse was busy with two lads playing pool and some sitting in small groups chatting amongst themselves. I waited for over an hour, and no one even said hello to me. I got up and walked out of the portacabin and never went back there.

When I next saw my psychiatrist, he made me an appointment to see a psychologist there. On the day of that appointment, I was out walking my dog when I realized I was supposed to be at the appointment. I rushed back to my car and drove straight there with my dog. He sat in the small psychologist's room with me, and she gave him a drink of water.

She chatted to me and asked me about my family and my past while taking notes in her notebook. She made an appointment for me to come back in a fortnight.

When I went back for my second appointment, she asked me what I wanted to talk about as I sat down. I said no, I was sent by my psychiatrist and if I knew why I was sent here, I could talk about it. She left my appointment open, and if I wanted to talk about anything, I could go back.

The whole idea had left me puzzled why I'd been sent there. Was it about my lack of eye contact or my paranoia? I never went back to see her again.

I had several support workers, and my next one was Jane; I spoke more about my illness to her than any other support worker I'd had, and it was Jane who was there for me when my dog had died. I found him when he was about 6 months old on some wasteland. He'd been through a lot with me. He was about fifteen and a half years old when I decided to have him put to sleep. I took him to the vets for one last time. It was a sad farewell. I was in tears, and I went to my Aunt Cath's to tell her my sad news.

I couldn't believe I'd lost him. Jane had given me her mobile phone number and said anytime I need to talk, or if I needed her, to call her. It was a weekend, and I rang her and told her the news. She wanted to come around to see me, but I said I was ok so she said she'd call round on Monday. I had him cremated and I still have to let his ashes go. I was in tears the whole weekend.

I also mentioned to Jane one weekend that I was drinking three 2-liter bottles of diet coke, 2 liters of milk and large amounts of tea and coffee. I complained of being thirsty all the time, and we discussed whether or not I was diabetic. I had a fasting blood test done earlier in that week and was awaiting the results.

It was at this time that Jane left as a support worker to manage the new Clubhouse. It had moved to the town center on Lord Street at the site of an old bank. Jane wanted me to go to the new Clubhouse because I lived in isolation. We said our farewells with a hug, and I was to go to Clubhouse when my referral came through.

I was at an outpatient appointment to see my psychiatrist (September 2004), and they told me my GP has been trying to get hold of me. My consultant told me I needed to go to the GP's office straight after my appointment. He said that I have diabetes so they would contact the office to let them know. He reviewed the antipsychotics I'd been taking and saw I'd been on Olanzapine since I had my relapse in 1998. Later, I found out that my schizophrenia and the Olanzapine had caused my diabetes. Because of this, my consultant changed my medication to Amisulpride, another antipsychotic medication.

The fasting blood test I had came back positive for diabetes, that is my HBA1c levels were high. My support worker said to me later that I took that well, but I just smiled at him and went on my way. I called at my GP's office, and to help control the diabetes, the doctor put me on two 500mg Metformin tablets, a Simvastatin tablet, and an Aspirin tablet to be dissolved in water. I had to go back for future appointments as they wanted to keep a check on my diabetes.

My assessment had come through for Clubhouse, the new one on Lords Street at the site of an old bank. I had a date on which to attend. It turned out as Jane already knew me, I didn't have to go through the risk assessment other service users had to before joining.

My new support worker took me and dropped me off there. I remember it was the Clubhouse Christmas party, and it wasn't the ideal introduction for someone who'd suffered a mental breakdown. I'd spent many years by myself not making eye contact with anyone. The first thing I said to Jane was that I am diabetic now.

"Yes, I heard. We were right then," She said.

I smiled to myself thinking back to how much fluid I was drinking then.

The building was full of service users, and I'd been thrown in at the deep end. The noise was overwhelming for me, and I wouldn't make eye contact with anyone in there.

"That's him."

"He can't stand up for himself."

"I won't go out with him as well."

"He's SAS too."

I realized (when Jane was my support worker) that it was stressful events and situations which caused me to hear more voices and my paranoia to get worse. These were the things that made me keep to myself.

Clubhouse was open Monday to Friday from around 10 am until 4 pm, and many service users with mental health problems went there. I took on far too much too soon by going every day and taking many of the courses. I earned certificates for these courses. I was soon settling in, yet sometimes when overwhelmed, I would make excuses not to go there.

You could help yourself to a coffee in the kitchen. Some service users just went in for a brew and to read the newspapers. They'd sit in a quiet room like they had on the wards of the psychiatric hospital. The quiet room was the old walk-in safe, having thick walls. They also had a smoke room which they soon closed a year or two later. It was only a little room and was later used as a storeroom.

They had computers with internet access available for us to use, a pool table, and a ping pong table.

It was January 2005, when I went for a diabetes check-up. My glucose levels were through the roof, and when the nurse said I'd not been taking my Metformin, I told her I had been. She went to see the GP and came back saying I must go to the hospital straight away as I had Ketones in my urine. She took me to see my GP in another room as I contacted my Aunt Cath to ask her if she could take me to Blackpool Outpatients right away. I went home, packed a bag, and waited for my aunt to come around to take me.

We arrived at the Outpatients, and I had to wait to see someone and also for a hospital bed. We sat there for some time, but my aunt had to get home. It was after she'd had gone that I got a bed on a diabetic ward and could settle in for the night.

It was the next day that I noticed the ward was full with some patients being diabetic and some not. The patient in the bed next to me did have diabetes. They checked the glucose levels of those with diabetes, and my levels were the highest on the ward.

I noticed the patient next to me eating chocolate, even drinking alcohol, which his wife brought to him, and his glucose levels were much lower than mine. It was only a week later that the consultant found out he was drinking a bottle of whisky a day. The consultant told him he was an alcoholic, but the guy was in denial.

The hospital gave me tablets for a week or two for my diabetes. At some point in the second or third week when they came to check my BM (blood glucose), I asked them why they didn't put me on insulin if the tablets aren't working. No one said anything. Not long after that, I was on daily insulin injections, and a diabetes specialist nurse took over my care. I knew then I would be on daily injections of insulin for the rest of my life.

I also had to see a dietician before I could go back home. They showed me how to use an insulin pen and how to inject myself. They told me the symptoms of hypoglycaemia – too low a level of blood sugar – and how to treat it. They also taught me how to look after my feet and gave me all this information in a folder.

After coming out of the hospital, I was given some good news that my schizophrenia was in remission. I had heard no voices while in the hospital, however, I still wasn't making eye contact with anyone. My paranoia had gone as hearing people talking about me had also stopped. The lack of eye contact remained the same. Every time I looked at people, they would look away from me.

The other news I got later that year was that I no longer needed a support worker. At some point later that year, they discharged me from the mental health team to come under the service of Clubhouse. A new manager was taking over there. A lot of new changes were to come, changes not only for me but for Clubhouse too.

My illness had taken away 15 to 20 years of my life, and I wanted my life back. I was ready for the world. I'd spoken to one of the Employment Officers for Lancashire County Council Employment Service around September 2005. Jane was still the manager of Clubhouse, at least for a little while yet. I told her I wanted to set up my own business as I had ideas on what to do, one being a dog walking business. The employment officer had told me to go to my local college and enroll in a business course they were running.

So, off I went on the enrollment day, to enroll for a business course at my local college. I drove there in my car and parked in the college parking lot. I was a little agitated about enrolling, so I sat in my car for ten minutes. When I felt comfortable enough, I went through the main doors and just focused on each step of the enrollment process.

The building was full of younger people all wanting to enroll. I never focused on what they were saying but concentrated on my plan I had in my head. I found directions to the room where I needed to go and made my way to the second floor. I soon found the tutor who was teaching the course, and I introduced myself to him.

He only asked me a few questions about my ideas for a business, and I passed them all. He said he was just taking names and details and if he had enough students, he would be in touch with me. I was happy with myself and how the enrolment went. I realized then that I'd forgotten to mention my illness to him.

He grabbed his pen and paper to take my name down, when I asked him, "If I had diabetes and schizophrenia would you see that as a problem?"

All of a sudden, he turned his back to me and started shuffling his papers as he sat there.

"I don't think this course is suitable for you." He finally responded.

"Sharon Pook advised me to enroll in this course," I said.

"Who's Sharon Pook?" He asked me.

I answered him, "My Employment Officer from Lancashire County Council Employment Service."

I asked him if he knew Peter Anderson who works at the college.

"No!" He said.

"I think you'd been illy advised." He huffed.

He was still sitting there with his back to me shuffling his papers. I got up to walk out, and when I looked back at him, he still sat with his back to me. I stood in the room's doorway, looking back one last time to see he still hadn't moved. I felt gutted!

I walked straight to my car and drove home in tears. I wasn't upset that he'd turned me down for the course but for how he treated me, sitting with his back to me, shuffling his papers. I phoned Clubhouse, and Joan, the support worker, answered. I told her what had happened. Then I spoke to Jane who asked me to come into Clubhouse to talk about it with her.

I drove down to Clubhouse, and with tears streaming, told her what had happened. Jane phoned the college to speak to them and find out who this tutor was. At first, they didn't know who the tutor was. After a few brews and some phone calls, the Clubhouse phone rang.

"We've got him," Jane said.

The college wanted me to discuss what had happened, but I wanted nothing to do with them. After talking with Jane, Joan wanted a meeting with them. That night, I'd written everything that had happened down while it was still fresh in my head.

The next day, someone came from the college, and we sat in the quiet room at the Clubhouse. I gave him the two sheets of paper where I'd written my account of what happened and explained to him what had happened on my enrollment day. I got no official apologies from them. That event plagued me for a long time and also taught me a lot about the discrimination and the way people treat mental health.

I'd tried to get back in the community, away from the protective bubble of the mental health services, after spending years to myself, but maybe I'd jumped in too soon. It was Stan, the new Clubhouse manager, who'd said that I should gradually expose myself to the community and workplace. I would always smile at the way he'd said it. The rub is there are times the community won't engage with people with mental illness because they don't take the time to understand the people living with it.

Stan had some great ideas which some would embrace and some not. One change was to get service users mixing with the public either back into work or volunteering. This was supposed to move service users on, helping them to a better life away from the day centers.

Diabetes can affect your mental health and vice versa, and in times of stress, it becomes harder to monitor and control. I had both diagnoses to work around. Any exercise meant a dip into the hypo range, and I was constantly struggling to get my diabetes under control. Diabetes is also a silent killer, and that's why I had all the appointments and check-ups.

Clubhouse had a new manager now. Stan brought new ideas, and sometime after my failure to enroll at college, I looked into volunteering. I met up with someone from the Blackpool Volunteer Centre, and they came to see me at Clubhouse. We sat and chatted about volunteering at Age Concern, one place looking for volunteers, and I went for an Induction course at the Fleetwood office.

Winter was on its way, and Age Concern wanted their winter packs ready for cold weather, all 500 of them. The packs contained a thermal mug, cup a soups, a fleece, and other items. I mainly packed them on my own with a little help from other volunteers. I was proving that after many years of not working, I still had it in me despite my breakdown.

I received a thank you card for all the hard work I did that week in putting together the winter packs for Aged Concern. It was a big morale booster for me, and when I mentioned it to Stan, he asked me if I'd kept the card to which I replied no.

I also applied to Lancashire County Council Adult and Community Services for a volunteer role with them. I had a home visit from Margret, a volunteer service officer, about my volunteering for them. She asked me about my schizophrenia so I told her about hearing voices. I also told her I'd tried to volunteer as a health walk leader and that they messed with me too much, so I gave that up. I got tired of driving the 30 miles only for no one to come for the walk.

Margret said she would have a chat with them as she has links with them through the council. I declined as I was looking for work with them, and she said she had a placement in mind for me with someone who enjoyed walking.

Margret was more worried about my diabetes than my mental health because I was on insulin, and I had frequent dips into hypoglycaemia. She said she would speak to her boss about that but that she had no concerns with the schizophrenia.

It was fortunate for me that my diabetes specialist nurse rang me when Margret was there. After I spoke to the nurse, Margret said she was ok with me volunteering while I had diabetes. She was also happy with the conversation between the nurse and me. She just had to pass it by her boss.

I got a phone call later that day from Margret informing me her boss said it was ok and that there were no worries regarding my diabetes or my volunteering with LCC.

One of the service users at Clubhouse had set up some courses there via the British Red Cross, and I also volunteered for them. He had a first aid course on Fridays which I attended every week. My life was getting busy, and Stan laughed when I said to him that I had to buy a diary to keep track of my schedule, volunteering, appointments, and my own interests.

The organizations I volunteered for didn't see my illness as a barrier although they knew my diagnosis. Even though it wasn't 8 am until 5 pm, 5 days a week, like paid work, I still had to commit to do the voluntary work. I had my induction for Lancashire County Council, held in the Making Space office in Bispham. I was not going to make the course as my car was in the garage for its annual safety inspection, but luck was on my side, and it got canceled. It was held a week or two later.

I'd found it very difficult to make eye contact with anyone at my induction as this was still very hard for me. Nobody on my care team had asked me about this before even though it was noticeable from the day I became ill in the 1990s. I wouldn't make eye contact with people, and no one asked me why. The truth is people wouldn't make eye contact with me for 17 years. Every time I made eye contact with someone, they would look away from me, and as a result, it became painful to even try.

I'd started taking a photography course at a college at St. Michaels on Wyre, and I'd drive to the college and back one evening a week. My enrollment to the college went well, and I stayed in the course for a few months.

One of my assignments was to photograph people or landscapes. As students, we had to vote on which to photograph. I voted for landscapes, but photographing people won the vote. I started getting stressed about having to photograph people and having to make eye contact with them through the lens of a camera.

The college said I could photograph landscapes but, I didn't want to differ from the other students or have the other students asking me why I could photograph landscapes. I finished the course a third of the way through just around the time my life came crashing down around me again.

I had ideas of coming off benefits and into self-employment. My visions for my future had failed. I was 45 and didn't want a life on benefits, of depending on the state. I have mental health issues, and trying to find a life between work and mental health is hard. I needed a balance in life. But when I overstretched that balance, I was back into psychosis and paranoia or living a life supported by the state handouts, maybe for the rest of my life.

Chapter 5

LCC Awards

My lack of eye contact with people over the years must have been noticeable, but no one ever mentioned it to me or my support team. I quit college because of it, and my plans for my future were no more. My plans to do outdoor photography and to come off benefits was another blow for me. But, as usual, I took it on the chin even though it was a blow to me I couldn't photograph people at college.

I had a new care co-ordinator, now Amanda, and I mentioned it to her and Stan at Clubhouse. My care co-ordinator made me an appointment with a psychologist at Mountcroft, but in the meantime, I was to carry on with my volunteering.

I'd been volunteering for LCC for a year, and it took me back when I received a phone call from Margret, my volunteer service organizer. She asked me if she could put me forward for the Lancashire County Council (LCC) local volunteer awards.

"Yes! You can put me forward for them," I said.

I was in tears when I rang Clubhouse to tell them the news.

"It's tears of joy, John," said Joan.

"Yes! I know," I responded.

With that, I tried to get back to my volunteering. Good stress will still sometimes affect me, and I can become agitated pacing up and down all night, not sleeping. Stressful events like this spin around in my head like a circle. I found this out when I went to college to learn to set up my business. I need time to myself to break the thoughts spiraling around in my head. It took me some time to learn how to do this. Reading a book or listening to my favorite music can break the spiraling circle for me.

I booked myself on a Safe Rambling course at Garstang Discovery Centre run by the local Mountain Rescue Team. They held it on a Sunday. It covered navigation and first aid and was followed by a walk from Garstang to Scorton and back practicing what we'd learned as we went. We stopped off at The Barn while at Scorton for a coffee and something to eat. I got through the entire day with no hypos. I was in my element; I loved it.

I had once done a 5-day survival course at Survival Aids near Penrith in the Lake District sometime in the 1980s. We had navigated with a button compass and slept out at just below zero degrees. I traveled by train to Penrith, but the train went straight past the station at Penrith. I got off at the wrong stop and caught the next train back to Penrith, but then I missed my pickup at the train station and started walking to Moorland. I was walking down dark country lanes when a car stopped, and the two ladies in the car offered to give me a lift to Moorland.

Thinking back, that's when I was getting agitated on public transport. Using a tram or bus into Blackpool and back made me very wary of people. Many a time, I would avoid public transport and walk to Blackpool, Cleveleys or into Poulton or further.

I often wonder when my schizophrenia started. I can remember when my world came crashing down around me but not exactly when it started. Schizophrenia can develop in childhood, and I could hear people saying things about me back then. I never put it down to voices in my head.

Now, I was yearning to get back outdoors and to study bushcraft again. I still had all my books in boxes, in drawers and in the two small bookcases I had purchased for them. Despite my difficulties, I was on the road to recovery and wanting to get back to my old hobbies and interests. Little did I know the struggle I would have achieving this.

I had a big sense of achievement after being put forward for my awards. Here I was taking someone out walking, a role I loved doing. I also offered to take others out walking, others who'd had the same issues as me.

No wonder Stan had laughed when I told him I had had to buy a diary to keep track of my work schedule. Here I was, having gone from social exclusion and living alone to a life where I am having to write my weekly schedule in a diary. My roles as a volunteer kept me busy, including when I helped the British Red Cross once or twice a week, but my mind was on the award and my lack of eye contact with people.

I had my appointment to see the psychologist at Mountcroft Resource Centre. Both Amanda and Stan attended the meeting with me. We didn't discuss the real reason as to why I wouldn't make eye contact with people which was that they looked down every time I tried.

We made a plan for me to work with Amanda on my progress. Within a week, I had switched to working on my progress with Stan at Clubhouse instead. While I was at

Clubhouse, I was to make eye contact with people at a distance, starting with Stan himself.

I'd spent 17 years not making eye contact with people, and I don't remember exactly when it happened, but it was some miracle that had taken place. Within three or four weeks, I was able to look people in the eye. I was given more good news when I heard I was shortlisted for the Local Pride Awards and could attend Lancaster University.

I traveled with Stan to Lancaster University for the Local Pride Awards ceremony. Stan had set his GPS for Lancaster University, but we still ended up in the wrong part of the university. We couldn't find anywhere to park, so Stan dropped me off as close as he could to the conference center where it was being held. He went off to find a place to park while I made my way into the center. I walked up a spiral staircase looking for the conference room. I asked some girls up there if they knew where the conference was, and they directed me back down the stairs. I followed the directions they'd gave me, and there it was on my right. When I entered the Conference Centre, I saw I was the first one there.

I phoned Margret to see if she'd gone in before me, but I only got her answering machine. Shortly after she arrived, we went in. I told the staff at the door that I had a guest because Stan hadn't arrived yet. Stan later thanked me for leaving his name with the staff at the door. He had ended up at the wrong conference center and was worried that I'd gone to the wrong one too.

As I sat with Margret wandering whether Stan would make it on time, the awards ceremony started. I began to feel funny and tested my blood glucose levels only to find I was hypo. I told Margret that I was hypo, and we went to the back of the room. I had three Hypo Fit 2 oat bars and a packet of glucose tablets. Margret struggled to open the sachets of Hypo Fit, but I'd managed to get them open.

Just as I was having my hypo episode, Stan arrived, and it wasn't long after that my name was called. I went up to collect the Local Area Pride Award that I'd won. I had my photo taken with Margret and Stan even though I was still recovering from my hypo when I went up for my award. I was worried about my sticky hands because as I'd opened the Hypo Fit, the sticky syrup used to treat low blood glucose had gotten on them.

When the awards were over, we had a cup of tea and something to eat. When we left, Margret gave us a lift to where Stan had parked his car, which was over on the other side of the university.

I'd received a Pride Award Certificate and a glass paperweight in the shape of a large diamond. When we got back to Clubhouse, I showed Joan my certificate and paperweight.

"I hope you're not going to put that away in a drawer," Joan said.

When I got back home, I put the paperweight in my bookcase, and the certificate went with all my other certificates in a plastic folder.

I kept busy and was soon surprised with some more good news. I was shortlisted for the Lancashire County Council Area Pride Awards. The awards were to be held in Chorley, and I would have to travel there. I asked Stan if he could take me, to which he said yes, but he'd need to ask his bosses first.

We traveled to a big hotel in Chorley just off the motorway.

We met Margret there, and Stan bought us a coffee while we sat waiting to go into the conference suite. As soon as the doors were open, we went in and sat at a huge round table. There were two other ladies at our table which I didn't know. I don't remember much of the occasion because I just focused on the table where we were placed. I was feeling a little agitated and stressed when they called me up.

I was given the top award, the Area Volunteer of The Year Award. I could see Stan and Margret standing and clapping their hands along with the rest of them in the room. I sat back down at the table and showed both Stan and Margret my award certificate and a presentation box they give me. Stan asked me what's in the box, but I didn't know.

"Have you've opened it yet?" Stan asked.

"No," I answered.

He surprised me when he responded, "Can I open it?" I told him he could.

It was a pen resting in the lining of the box, which I still have today along with the framed certificate I received with it.

After the awards, we were all treated to a meal by Lancashire County Council. I enjoyed the day, and when it was over, Stan took me back to Fleetwood to my flat. My comfort zone had been broken by having to accept my award in front of all those people. It was a far cry from my days of social Isolation.

Next, I was invited by the Lancashire County Council to attend a conference at the Guild Hall in Preston. It was to be an evening event, and, once again, Stan came with me. It reminded me of the House of Parliament in London which I'd seen on television. It had large corridors and big leather seats. We sat in one of the large rooms and had a buffet before going into the conference meeting. Margret attended too as it was an occasion not to be missed.

I felt proud of winning both awards and asked Margret if I could help any other service user under the volunteer service. Margret was pleased I'd asked her because she had an elderly gent in mind. He was a blind chap, and I would visit him to make him a drink, have a chat, and read him his mail.

I started to look for some part-time work so I went back to Lancashire County Council Employment Service. I was assisted by an Employment Officer there to help me find work. We looked at a few jobs over the coming months, and one job did stand out, that of a janitor and assistant caretaker at a Medical Centre not far from where I lived. My employment officer had known of the post, and I agreed to fill in the application form.

It wasn't long after sending the form in that they wanted me to come in for an interview, and my employment officer joined me at the interview. My role would be to open and close the center along with some cleaning and assistant caretaker duties. I was to start the job within a week's time and have a month-long trial.

I was pleased to get the job after many years unemployed on sickness benefits. It was an early morning start, and then I'd to go back in the evenings to lock up. I was shown the ropes by my supervisor during the first week or two while he helped me learn the duties.

I cleared bags and bags of rubbish from the parking lot and adjoining grounds. It was hard work, and I could feel my legs aching from the 20-hour a week job. Even with the aching legs, I was grateful for the job.

I'd also started reading my outdoor books again. I'd started writing, including writing notes on my recovery process. I hoped that someday I could put it in a book to help others understand and gain insight into Paranoid Schizophrenia.

Chapter 6

Moving Forward

I'd met a girl that lived over near Manchester, and we'd kept in contact via telephone. We talked about meeting up so I drove to a café over near Manchester to meet her. She let me buy her a coffee, and we talked about my job at the medical center. Before we met up, I told her that I had Paranoid Schizophrenia, and when she wanted to talk more about it at the café, I told her this probably isn't the right place to talk about it. She agreed so we said our goodbyes.

I kept in contact with her for a week or two over the phone, but then she texted me to say it was all going too fast for her. She called it off. I put it all down to a learning curve for me and that I was pushing her too fast.

I started to become agitated, not sleeping at night, and having suicidal thoughts when I couldn't sleep. Finding a balance between work, hobbies, and life can be hard for someone with mental illness.

As luck would have it, I was offered a week's holiday with full pay even though I'd never mentioned anything at work about the fact that I had been struggling.

Within a week, I was feeling refreshed and ready to start back at work, however, it wasn't long before it all started happening again. Because of this struggle to hold down my job, I made an appointment with the Disability Employment Adviser at the Job Centre Plus Office.

I was in tears at my appointment as I told her I wasn't coping too well in my job. I had holes in my shoes that I'd not noticed and a serious blister on my foot. I wasn't looking after my personal care, struggling with my washing and shaving. She told me I needed to give up my job and go back on sickness benefits.

I drove back home and phoned Margret, my volunteer officer, to tell her I was struggling. I was in tears again as she told me I needed to phone my supervisor and tell him I am not well. I knew I wasn't getting any better, but I didn't want to end up back on sickness benefits. I phoned my supervisor anyway to tell him I couldn't continue with my job, and he understood, saying he'd go in and take over for me.

The job had taken so much out of me both mentally and physically, and it took me some time to recover from it. Later, I started having a hard time with my volunteer work. I finished as a volunteer with Lancashire County Council.

I even lacked motivation to do my personal care, washing, shaving, and having baths.

I'd stopped driving and gave up my car.

Before giving up my car, I'd been traveling to a drop-in center in Cleveleys called the Lighthouse. I was going there two or three times a week, and they wanted me to continue going there by tram.

It was about a 20-minute ride on the tram, and after some weeks, I started getting paranoid that people were following me. I was finding it hard using public transport again, so I started using taxis to get to where I needed to go.

One day, I opened my front door to a guy who was selling internet and phone packages. I told him that I wasn't feeling too well and that I wasn't interested. He then asked me for a glass of water, which I gladly went to get him, and when I came back with it, he entered my flat.

Then, his mate arrived in my flat trying to sell me a phone package deal. I was getting more agitated and tried to ask them to leave. However, he was distracting me with questions while the other was signing me up for a deal.

"Is that a Meercat on the window ledge?" He pointed to my ornament.

"Yes," I replied.

"Can I have another glass of water?"

It seemed ages, and the only way I could get them out of my flat was to sign up for a package which I did.

As I managed to get them to leave, I heard the lad say to his mate, "How easy was that, Eh!"

I rang the Lighthouse to tell them what had just happened, and I went there to see the manager about it. She was soon on the phone to the company to cancel the contract and put in a complaint.

They apologized and asked if I knew the name of the representatives, which I didn't. I told them I didn't want to put in a complaint because it would just put more stress on me.

I was also back on the books at Mountcroft Resource Centre with a new support worker called Alan. He would visit me to see how I was getting on and if I needed any help.

After about two or three years, I met a lady called Lilly Donovan, a retired nurse living in Wales. Lilly had spent many years as a nurse working at a hospital in Manchester. She'd worked long day and night shifts and had a son, daughter, and two grandsons.

We'd texted and often phoned each other, but I couldn't travel to Wales to meet her because of my paranoia on public transport. Lilly wasn't concerned about this when she talked about us meeting up. She asked about coming to Fleetwood for a few days, but most of all she accepted me and my Schizophrenia.

I'd had an appointment to see the Disability Employment Adviser again so she could see how I was getting on. When I went to meet her, she mentioned an organization called Positive Futures. It was a bit like other services I'd been to in the past, helping people who had or have a serious illness of some kind. They made an appointment for me to see Sarah from Positive Futures the following week.

When I went to see Sarah, I was feeling a little agitated and nervous. Sarah seemed bright with a positive attitude which put me at ease, and she listened to me as I talked about myself and my Schizophrenia.

I agreed to go on one of their courses they were setting up in Fleetwood. The course was one day a week for about 6 to 8 weeks. In the course, I talked about my experience with Schizophrenia, and I was struck by some of the other people's stories there.

Lilly wanted to come and visit me for the first time. She'd arranged to travel by train and to arrive at Poulton train station where I would meet her. That would've been a long journey by train for me, lasting almost a day.

I arrived by taxi to meet her at Poulton train station, and I can still picture Lilly getting off the train. There were lots of school kids catching the trains home, and there were lots of other people getting on and off the train.

I couldn't see Lilly right away because of all the confusion, but there she was walking towards me. She smiled, and we kissed. We then made our way off the platform to catch a taxi back to my flat.

The next day, I showed Lilly around town, and we went to Freeport Shopping Village. I took Lilly to see both my aunts. I wasn't used to having someone stay with me, especially having spent many years on my own. I thought I may struggle with her company because of my mental illness, but I liked her.

Lilly stayed for a week before going back to Wales and traveled a few times after that to see me again. I agreed to go with her to Wales the next time and meet her family.

The next time Lilly came down for a week to stay, we met both my sisters at a café in Fleetwood so she could get to know them. Both my sisters were pleased I'd met someone after all these years of ill health.

I'd also shown my sisters this book I was writing, and one of them started crying when she read my script. It must've been a shock for them both to read it from first-hand as to what I'd been through. I'd never spoken about my illness before in such detail, let alone write about it.

After Lilly spent another week in Fleetwood, we then got a taxi to Poulton train station to travel to Wales to meet her family. It was a short train ride from Poulton to Manchester, and we sat at Costa café waiting for our next train while having a coffee and a bite to eat.

As we sat at the station café, I felt agitated and nervous at the thought of traveling by train. It was a busy and noisy environment. I felt out of my comfort zone as we waited for our next train to Wales and watched the people rushing by to catch their trains, supping drinks, and eating sandwiches.

When we got on the train to Wales, Lilly held my hand, as if to say, 'it's OK. I am here.' It was noisy and stressful for me, but after a few hours journey, we were in Wales. When we arrived in Lilly's hometown, we had a 15-minute walk to her home.

I spent a week getting to know Lilly's son, his partner, and Lilly's two grandsons. We walked along the seafront where we would stop for a coffee and to people watch. People watching was something Lilly introduced me to and is widely known in Wales.

We caught the train back to Fleetwood, and Lilly stayed a few days before she returned back to Wales. We kept in touch by phone or Messenger.

When I got a message in Messenger from a lady asking me if I was the brother of Andrew Debar, my world came crashing down again.

My brother, Andrew, had moved to Australia some years before, and I checked with my sister, Louise, to see if she knew this woman. Louise confirmed she was Andrew's ex-partner.

I messaged her back to see why she was contacting me only to find out it was that Andrew had passed away in his sleep. Andrew was the youngest in the family. He was at work when he decided to go home because he had stomach pains. They found out after he'd died that he had bowel Cancer. I had to contact my other siblings and relatives to tell them the sad news, but little did I know how this would have an effect on me.

I ceased contact with Lilly and even stopped messaging her. I stopped eating and looking after myself. After a few days, there was a knock on my door. I didn't feel like answering, but when I did, it was Lilly. I'd remembered in our last conversation that I had mentioned my brother passing away.

I was unshaven, unkempt, and hadn't had a bath for over a week. When I let her in, it dawned on me how much she must love me. Lilly had traveled all this way to see me, and she never told me she was coming here.

Lilly told me to get a bath and shave while she cleaned up my flat. After I had a bath or shower, I had something to eat. We talked a long while and even talked about the subject of marriage. It was then that it came to me. I'd found what I've been looking for all my life and that was to settle down with the right woman. Here Lilly was, the right woman for me.

I got down on one knee and asked her for her hand in marriage.

"Yes," she replied, and then we kissed.

The next day we walked into town and had a coffee at a café. We couldn't believe I asked her for her hand in marriage, and I asked her again to which she replied "Yes" once more.

When Lilly traveled back to Wales, I met up with Anne and Louise, my sisters. We went to our mum and dad's grave to say farewell to Andrew. Then we walked to the seafront to let a balloon off for our younger brother. The balloon couldn't take flight, and it only took to the air after several attempts. Anne couldn't stop laughing because Louise kept getting my name mixed up with Andrew's name.

We'd said our farewells to Andrew, and now I came back home to make our wedding plans. Lilly had asked me if I wanted to go on holiday with them at Haven Holiday Park in the Lake District. It had been years since I last went on a holiday, and I said yes! I would love to go with them.

Our wedding plans were put on hold as Lilly traveled to Fleetwood a few days before our holiday. A few days later we caught the train to Grange-Over-Sands where it was picked up at the train station there.

They'd hired two caravans there, and some nights we'd have the grandchildren over with us.

The last time I'd been away was in the 1980s on a 5-day survival course in the Lake District, but here I was, in 2015, having a week's holiday in a caravan with Lilly and her family. I couldn't help thinking that a couple of years ago this wouldn't have been possible because of my illness. I knew I'd come a long way and that I was doing well to be able to go on holiday with Lilly. At the end of the week, her family drove back to Wales while she and I caught the train back to Fleetwood.

Making plans to get married can be a stressful event, and I would be moving to a new life in Wales too. I wondered how my Schizophrenia would be with all these changes. I kept busy sorting out my belongings in getting ready for the move to Wales after our wedding. Alan helped me by taking stuff to the tip and charity shops.

With Lilly in Wales and me in Fleetwood, we were both busy organizing our wedding. Our venue was going to be at the Euston Hotel, and we were to have it all take place there.

My aunt Cath had phoned me to say she'd seen a death notice in the newspaper. It was my Aunt Rennie, my mum's sister, who'd passed away. Her funeral was in Fleetwood, and I went with my aunt Cath to say my farewell. It was on my way out that I passed my uncle and two cousins. I briefly spoke to them before leaving.

When I got outside, someone came running after me shouting, "John." I turned around and said, "Yes?"

It was a guy who had attended the funeral. He asked me if I wanted to go back to the wake at the Euston Hotel, and I said I would.

I asked my Aunt Cath if she wanted me to take her home on the bus, and she'd said no, she'd be OK by herself. I waited around in town so that I could go to the Euston Hotel later that afternoon. It was while I was walking around the town center that I bumped into another cousin, and we got to chatting about my wedding. It was then that I heard him say, "It'll be a bad move, you moving to Wales."

Am I still hearing voices from people? Why would it be a bad move for me to move to Wales? I couldn't believe what I was hearing. Why he would say such a thing? I decided to walk home contemplating on what he'd said. Things were going well for me. Why can't he be happy for me? Maybe it's not voices? I did speak to Lilly and my Aunt Cath, but I decided to forget about it and carry on with our wedding.

My aunt Betty was now in a care home, and I'd often visit her with Lilly. It was sad to see her in there, but she'd visited me when I was in the psychiatric ward. It's not a good place to be in a care home away from your family, however, her family would visit her every day. I invited Aunt Betty to the wedding, but sadly she couldn't make it on the day.

I'd invited family and friends along with Stan, Joan, and Alan. Lilly had invited her family and friends also.

I was to spend the night before our wedding at the Euston Hotel. Lilly stayed at the Premier Inn in Bispham with her family. Lilly had to endure the night without any air conditioning, and it was after the wedding that we realized she could've spent the night at the Euston Hotel in a different room.

There was no Stagg night for me! I spent the night at the Euston Hotel. There was a wonderful view out of my room window as I could see across the bay to the Forest of

Bowland hills. I went to the hotel bar to have a drink and chat with Lilly's daughter before I retired back to my room.

I was watching TV most of the night and texting Lilly to see how she was. I finally did get some sleep and woke up early that day. We never talked on our wedding day, but we did text each other when we woke up.

I went down for breakfast with Lilly's daughter, and then I had a shave and shower before putting on my best suit. I was too busy welcoming our guests to be worried. I was trying not to think about walking down the wedding aisle.

My sister, Anne, was helping sort out the venue, but she was running late and hadn't arrived. We were having a butterfly theme to our wedding, and I began worrying that it wouldn't all be ready for when Lilly arrived. Soon, Anne and Lilly's friends came and began to get the venue ready.

At about 2 pm, we were all ready. I was waiting with my uncle as my best man for Lilly to come. It seemed an eternity waiting for her.

I thought back to my days of being unwell and hearing voices.

"That's him."

Then I'd hear someone say, "Defense mode, Knowles."

They were obviously voices in my head, but thinking about that call to be alert helped me block out everyone in the room. When Lilly came walking down the aisle, I focused on my wife to be.

Her oldest grandson was carrying our wedding rings on a cushion, and as he handed them over to the best man, the best man dropped the rings on the floor.

We were both nervous as we said our wedding vows in front of all our guests. We kissed and were asked to kiss three times. After we'd had our photographs taken, we all headed to the dining room for a meal and evening reception. It'd been a long day, and I'd been on my feet the whole time so I was glad to finely have a sit down.

I mixed with the guests thanking them for coming. I spoke to Louise and her family. She asked me who the poet in the hat was.

"Poet"! I thought.

"Where?" I asked.

"No, that's not a poet; it's Stan from Clubhouse." I replied.

Next to Stan was Joan, who also works at Clubhouse, and next to her was Alan, my support worker. Some of our guests were beginning to leave, and the remaining guests wanted to dance.

It's customary for the bride and groom to have the first dance, but this had never crossed my mind before this moment.

'I am not a dancer.'

'I have two left feet.'

'But I've come this far now.' I thought to myself.

We got up to have our first dance, and then other guests joined us on the dance floor. It was an hour or two after our dance that we retired up to our room.

The next day, we woke up husband and wife. We had our breakfast with Lilly's daughter and then made our way to Poulton train station to leave for our honeymoon in York. After we spent a week in York, we arrived back in Fleetwood ready for my move to Wales.

Lilly stayed in Fleetwood for a few days before heading back to Wales while I was to follow on in a day or two. Louise's partner knew of someone who could move my belongings to Wales, and he could also take me with him in his van. This would save me having to find my own way to Wales.

Louise and Anne were to sort out the rest of my belongings that I left behind. They were also to going to give my flat a good cleaning and hand my keys in to the Housing Association.

On the day of my move to Wales, the removal man arrived with another lad to help him. He'd turned up two hours early and was waiting outside in his van. He told me that he couldn't do any lifting because he had a bad back, and he turned out to be a bit grumpy too.

I started to worry about traveling in the van with him. He was asking for more money, but we'd already agreed on a price and shook hands on it. I had also agreed that he could have my cooker, upright fridge/freezer, and double bed.

Luckily, Louise and her partner had arrived along with her son and his dad. They were all there to help load the van.

Then Anne arrived with her partner, and they said they'd drive me to Wales. It turned out to be a relief that I wouldn't have to travel with the removal men. I said my goodbyes to Louise and promised to keep in touch with her.

As we got in the car, Anne said she'd made a flask of coffee and some sandwiches which took me back to our childhood days when we traveled around Scotland. The journey had taken us over two hours with stops for the toilets and more coffee and sandwiches.

The removal men had arrived before us, and by the time we got there, they were already unloading. They must've stopped off to pick up a young girl to help us because there were three of them now.

When we arrived, I helped the lad, the removal man's helper, move my washer/dryer up a flight of stairs into the house. However, as we were coming up the steps, I collapsed under the weight of the appliances. I managed to get myself back up, and although I'd crushed my engagement ring, I was able to get it off my finger. Then, I checked my blood glucose level and found it was high at over 25mmoll. I used a correction dose of quick-acting insulin to bring it back down.

When they brought the wardrobe in, they'd left it in the hall, and I said to the lad that needed to go upstairs.

"No, we can't go upstairs." He replied.

They left it in the hallway while everything else had gone in the downstairs middle room. When the removal men had gone, Anne and her partner moved the wardrobe upstairs.

They both stayed for a drink and a bite to eat before saying farewell and heading back home to Lancashire. When I closed the front door, I closed it on an old life in Fleetwood and opened a new door to a new married life in Wales.

After Thoughts

Schizophrenia is a serious mental illness, and like many illnesses, it can take your life away. I lost 20 years of my life to schizophrenia.

I can remember those 17 years when I had lack of eye contact with people, even my relatives and friends. Today, I can maintain eye contact with people as well as hold a conversation with them.

In 2004, I changed my life around, but I always had a fixed vision and goal. I wanted not only to get better but to also settle down with someone. I wanted a new life in Scotland, where I'd spent some of my childhood days.

Many a time, I've had to pick myself up along my recovery. Today, I am happily married with two grandsons I call my own, a step-son and step-daughter, and a wonderful wife. Most importantly, I've found my vision and goal and settled down to a new life in Wales.

My goals have now moved on to newer ones. My schizophrenia may never go away and may follow me wherever I go. I manage the best I can, still taking some steps back, while I am still moving forward in life.

I wouldn't say I've had an adventurous life. In fact, I missed out on life. I am moving forward, and at the same time, I'm reclaiming the visions I had in the 1980s before my schizophrenic breakdown.

Sadly, both my aunties have now passed away, and I hold them both dearly in my heart.